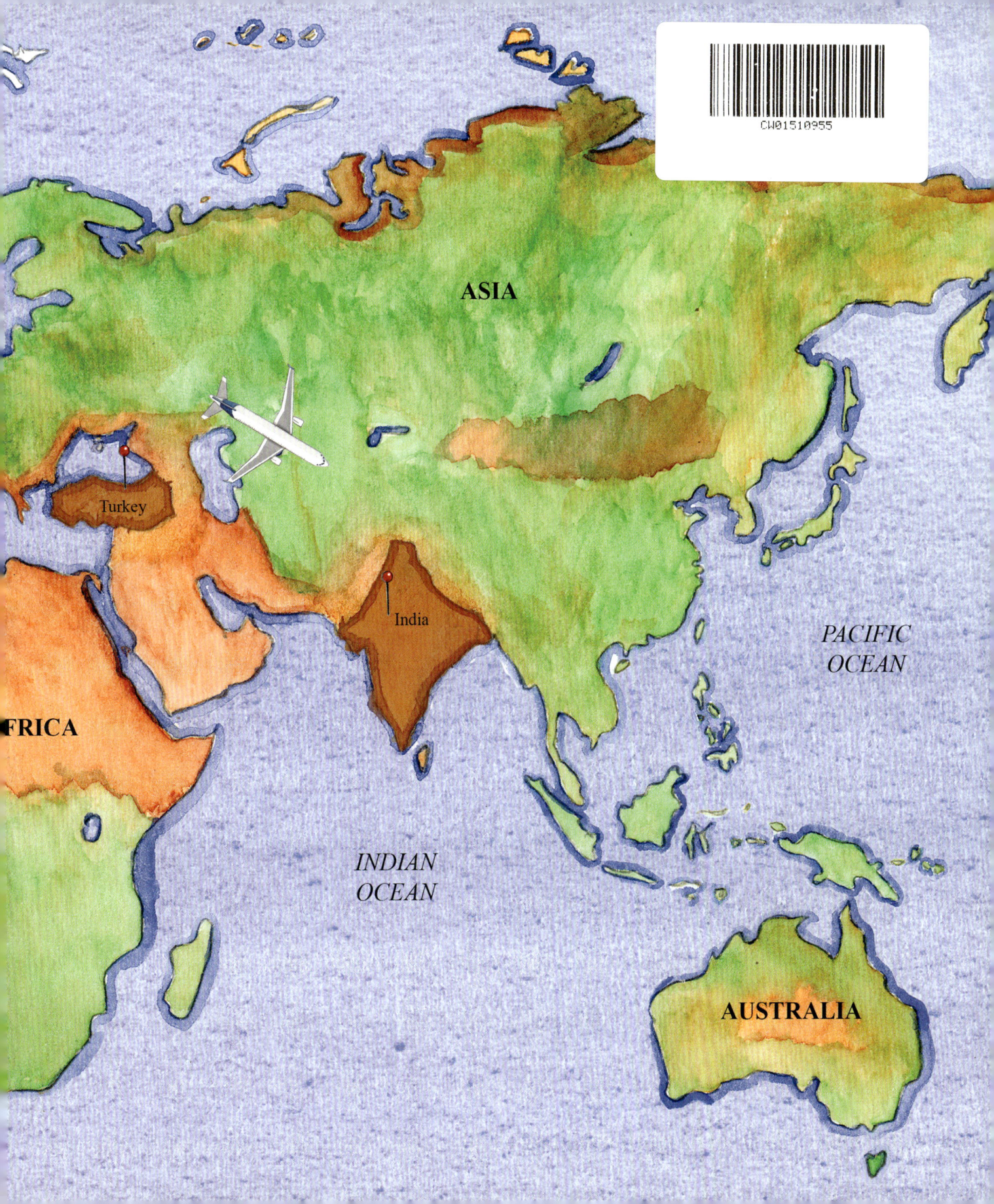

HALIMA SHALA EBRAHIM

ADNAN'S TRAVELS

ILLUSTRATIONS BY TRACEY TURNER

© 1437 AH/2016 CE Halima Shala Ebrahim

First Published in September 2017 by
Ta-Ha Publishers Ltd.
Unit 4, The Windsor Centre
Windsor Grove, West Norwood
London, SE27 9NT, UK
www.tahapublishers.com
support@tahapublishers.com

Written by: Halima Shala Ebrahim
Illustrated by: Tracey Turner
Book Design by: Zaahir Khan
Edited by: Aisha Wright

A catalogue record of this book is available from the British Library.

ISBN: 978 1 84200 163 9

Printed and bound by: IMAK Ofset, Turkey

Acknowledgements
Shaykh Dr. Abdalqadir As-Sufi

For all the children I love who inspire me to tell stories,
for my husband, a fellow traveller
and for the best storyteller I had, my father

AFGHANISTAN

CHINA

SRINAGAR

Indus

PAKISTAN

• AMRISTAR

NEW DELHI

NEPAL

Himalayas

JAIPUR

AGRA

LUCKNOW

• KANPUR

BANGLADESH

AJMER

Ganges

• AHMADABAD

• SURAT

INDIA

CALCUTTA•

• NAGPUR

HYDERABAD

Bay of Bengal

MUMBAI

Arabian Sea

• GOA

CHENNAI

PONDICHERRY

• KOCHI

Indian Ocean

KOVALAM

SRI LANKA

Dear Mum,

We've arrived safely in India! The flight from London was so long, we were really tired. We were met at the airport by Dad's friend, Uncle Feroz. He had a wide, white turban and Dad recognised him immediately even though there were lots of people dressed like him.

Uncle Feroz took us to his apartment which is near the university where he teaches. The streets were so busy. Buses, cars, **tuk tuks**, and wandering cows and buffalo fill the roads - you have to see it to believe it! There are crowds of people, and the drivers hoot their horns so much that the noise made me dizzy. Eventually we had a meal of curries, **naan** bread and delicious mango **lassi**, and felt very much at home.

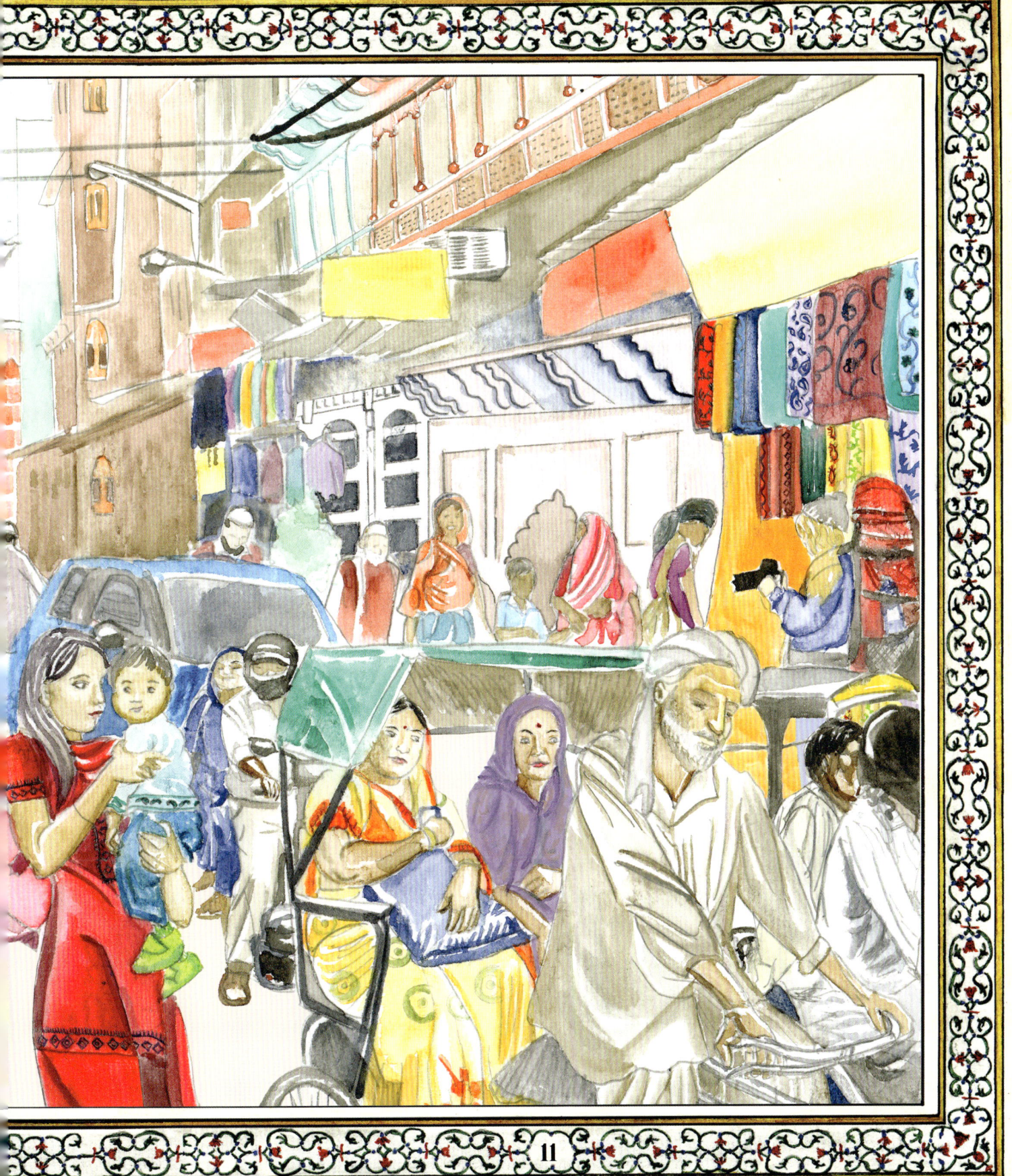

On Thursday night, Uncle Feroz hosted a **dhikr** with his friends. One of them, Izmet, has a famous **Qawwali** group.

The men played some drums, and Izmet sang what they call 'naats', which are beautiful songs praising our Prophet, **sallallahu 'alayhi wa sallam**. I've heard Dad play them on CDs, but it was so different hearing it live - my heart felt it could leap out of my body! I didn't understand the **Urdu**, but Dad explained some of the words.

We walked along **Chandni Chowk** which is an old road lined with shops that lead into a maze of streets and alleyways. It was built by Jehanara, the daughter of the great **Moghul** ruler, Shah Jehan. Long ago, wealthy people helped the locals by building them schools, roads, hospitals and places to feed the poor. These places were all **waqafs**.

We went to the Red Fort and the Jama Masjid of Delhi which were close by. The mosque is enormous! 30,000 people can pray inside.

We also went to **Nizamuddin Auliya's** tomb where we found crowds of people visiting and reciting **Fatiha.**

We spent the next few days exploring the city of Delhi. We learnt about the great Moghuls who had ruled India and built amazingly beautiful palaces and gardens.

We visited the Shalimar Gardens. Our guide told us that parrots and pairs of peacocks used to roam wild there, and terraces, waterfalls and canals used to flow through them.

Yesterday we went to Agra to explore the Taj Mahal. Shah Jehan built it as a tomb for his wife Mumtaz. Its marble was transported from distant quarries by elephants, and the precious and semiprecious stones that decorate it came from Tibet and **Ceylon**.

Tomorrow we're flying to Istanbul. I'll miss all the **mithai** - **burfi** is my favourite! I'm sending you the recipe for mango lassi. It's so easy to make and really delicious.

Love, Adnan

ROMANIA

RUSSIA

BULGARIA

Black Sea

GREECE

GEORGIA

Istanbul

Samsun

Trabzon

ARMENIA

Euphrates

Eskisehir

Ankara

Karakose

Aegean Sea

TURKEY

Lake Van

IRAN

Izmir

Konya

Tigris

Gaziantep

Diyarbakir

CYPRUS

SYRIA

Mediterranean
Sea

LEBANON

IRAQ

ISRAEL

JORDAN

LIBYA

EQYPT

SAUDI ARABIA

Dear Mum,

I LOVE travelling! We landed in Istanbul last night and went straight to our hotel opposite the Hagia Sophia which is a famous museum. At **Fajr** I heard so many **adhans** that I lost count.

This morning, on our way to visiting the tomb of the famous **Companion** of the Prophet, Ayub al-Ansari, Dad explained how all the Companions wanted to conquer Constantinople for the Muslims since the Prophet, sallallahu 'alayhi wa sallam, said that whoever did so would be with him in the Garden. Many tried, but a 19 year-old called Muhammad Fatih devised a brilliant strategy and after a long battle he succeeded. He renamed the city 'Istanbul'.

We walked to the Sultan Ahmad Mosque which the tourists call the 'Blue Mosque' because of all its blue tiles inside. It has lots of enormous chandeliers which light up the interior. There are so many magnificent mosques and buildings and a lot of them look alike. Uncle Mehmet said it's because a famous architect called **Sinan** designed many of them.

There's a tram here and it's a really exciting way to travel. Dad's friend Mehmet came to give us a tour of the city. Later we went to a sweet shop and I bought you a whole box so you can taste as many goodies as I have! I've noticed that everyone drinks tea here. Throughout the day the shopkeepers constantly offer us tea or juice. My favourite is apple tea

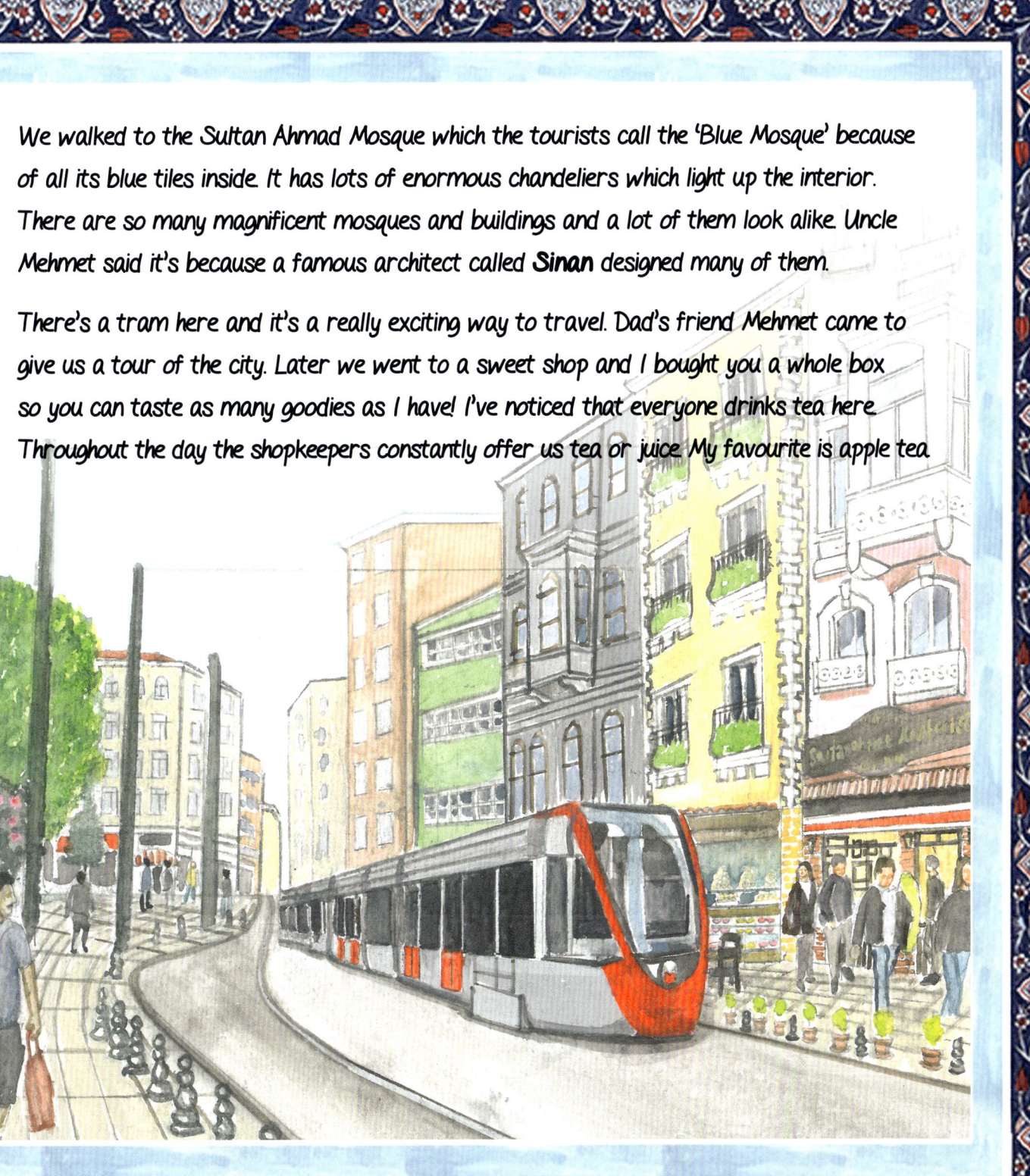

We spent some time in the Grand Bazaar and I have never seen so many shops in one space. There are avenues of gold shops, leather, pottery, jewellery, clothes shops and more - there's so much choice!

Over a delicious kebab lunch, we looked forward to visiting Topkapi which was once a huge palace complex from where the Ottoman sultans ruled. Dad explained that there are lots of treasures in a special room, including big swords of the **Sahaba**. I can't wait to see them!

Later in the afternoon we visited the 1492 Museum which tells of Constantinople's conquest. It has lots of paintings depicting the battle but the most exciting thing is the exhibition of powder kegs and cannons.

Dad told me that Istanbul is partly in Europe and partly in Asia, and we took a ferry across the **Bosphorus** from the European side to the Asian side

Dad treated us to a Turkish bath. It wasn't actually a bath, more like a sauna, and much better than the one at the gym.

We met with a **calligrapher** who showed us his work and I chose one to bring home which was embossed with real gold.

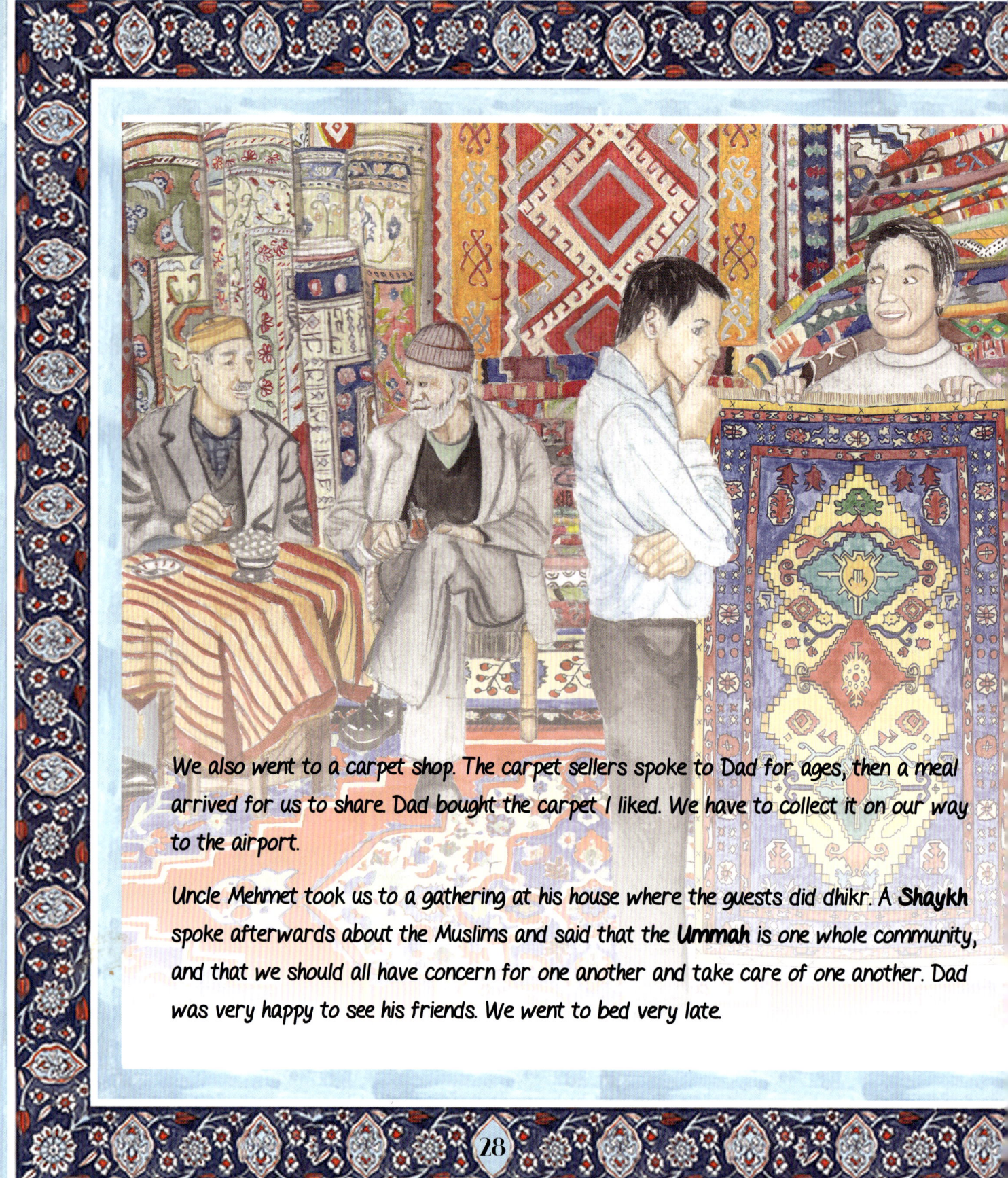

We also went to a carpet shop. The carpet sellers spoke to Dad for ages, then a meal arrived for us to share. Dad bought the carpet I liked. We have to collect it on our way to the airport.

Uncle Mehmet took us to a gathering at his house where the guests did dhikr. A **Shaykh** spoke afterwards about the Muslims and said that the **Ummah** is one whole community, and that we should all have concern for one another and take care of one another. Dad was very happy to see his friends. We went to bed very late.

We took a short flight to the ancient city of Konya to visit **Mawlana Jalal ad-Din ﷺ's** tomb. He lived about 800 years ago. Uncle Mehmet's friend Reza met us and showed us around. The town was full of visitors and we even got to see the Prime Minister of Turkey while we were watching the Whirling **Dervishes** perform.

Love, Adnan

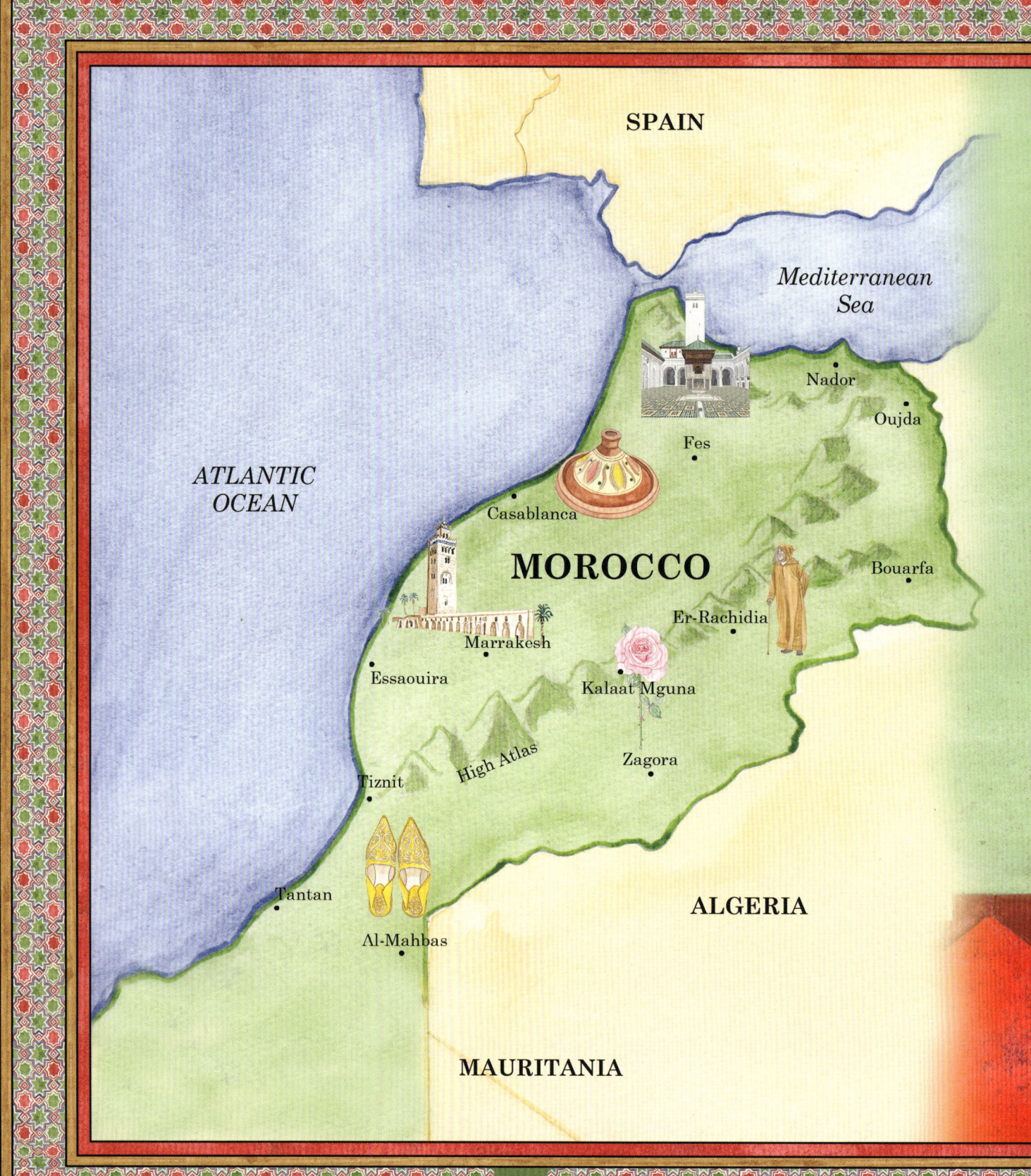

SPAIN

*Mediterranean
Sea*

*ATLANTIC
OCEAN*

Nador

Oujda

Fes

Casablanca

MOROCCO

Bouarfa

Er-Rachidia

Marrakesh

Essaouira

Kalaat Mguna

Tiznit

High Atlas

Zagora

Tantan

ALGERIA

Al-Mahbas

MAURITANIA

Dear Mum,

I was very happy to see Shaykh Abdullah at the airport when we arrived in Casablanca, the largest city in Morocco. I remembered his visit to us last year. He greeted us with such a huge smile and hug, as well as lots of kisses on my head.

He took us to his apartment where his family welcomed us with a big feast. We sat around a huge platter of couscous and lamb, and ate from either side. You'll be glad to hear that we gave his wife all the gifts you sent and she was very happy.

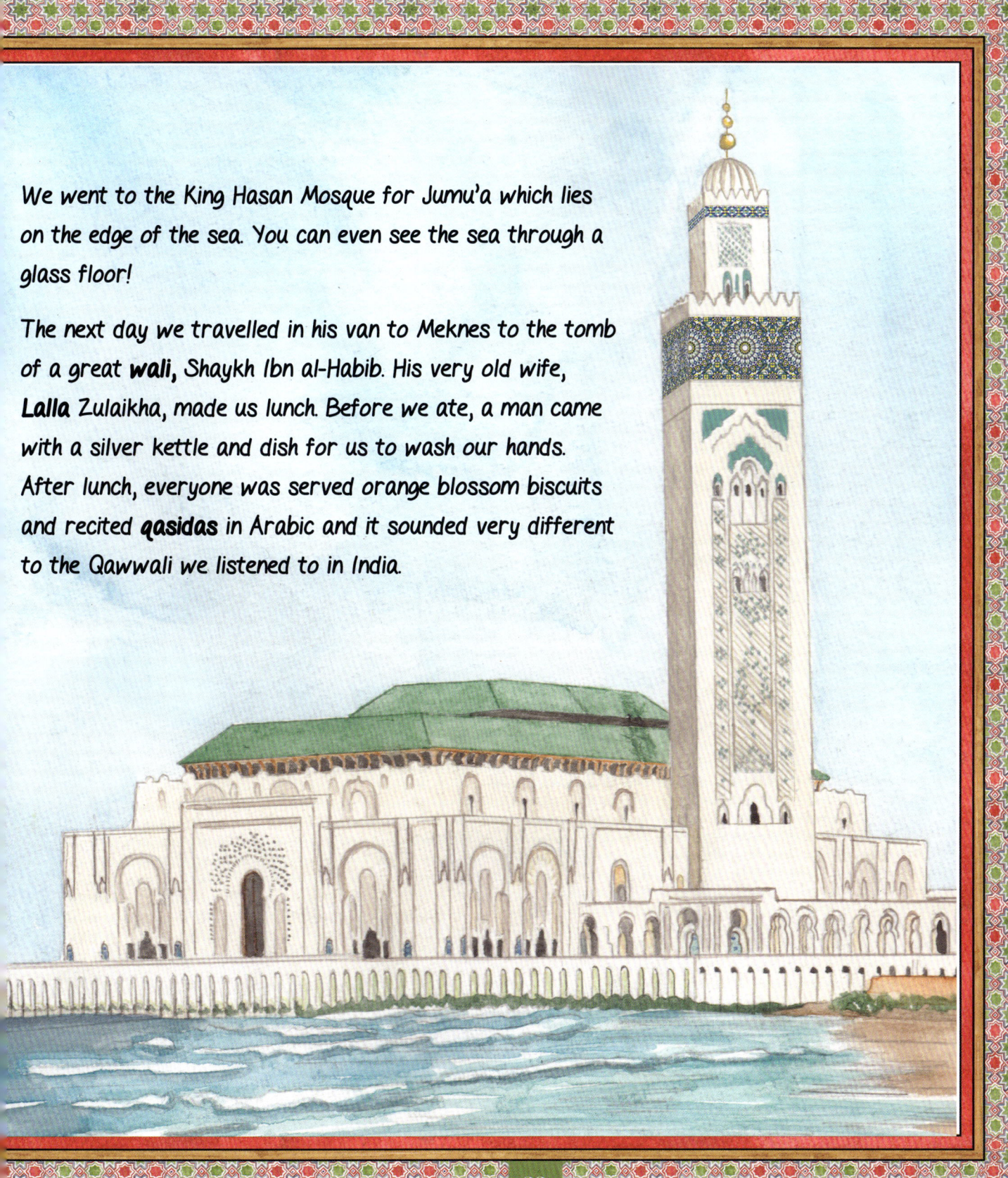

We went to the King Hasan Mosque for Jumu'a which lies on the edge of the sea. You can even see the sea through a glass floor!

The next day we travelled in his van to Meknes to the tomb of a great **wali,** Shaykh Ibn al-Habib. His very old wife, **Lalla** Zulaikha, made us lunch. Before we ate, a man came with a silver kettle and dish for us to wash our hands. After lunch, everyone was served orange blossom biscuits and recited **qasidas** in Arabic and it sounded very different to the Qawwali we listened to in India.

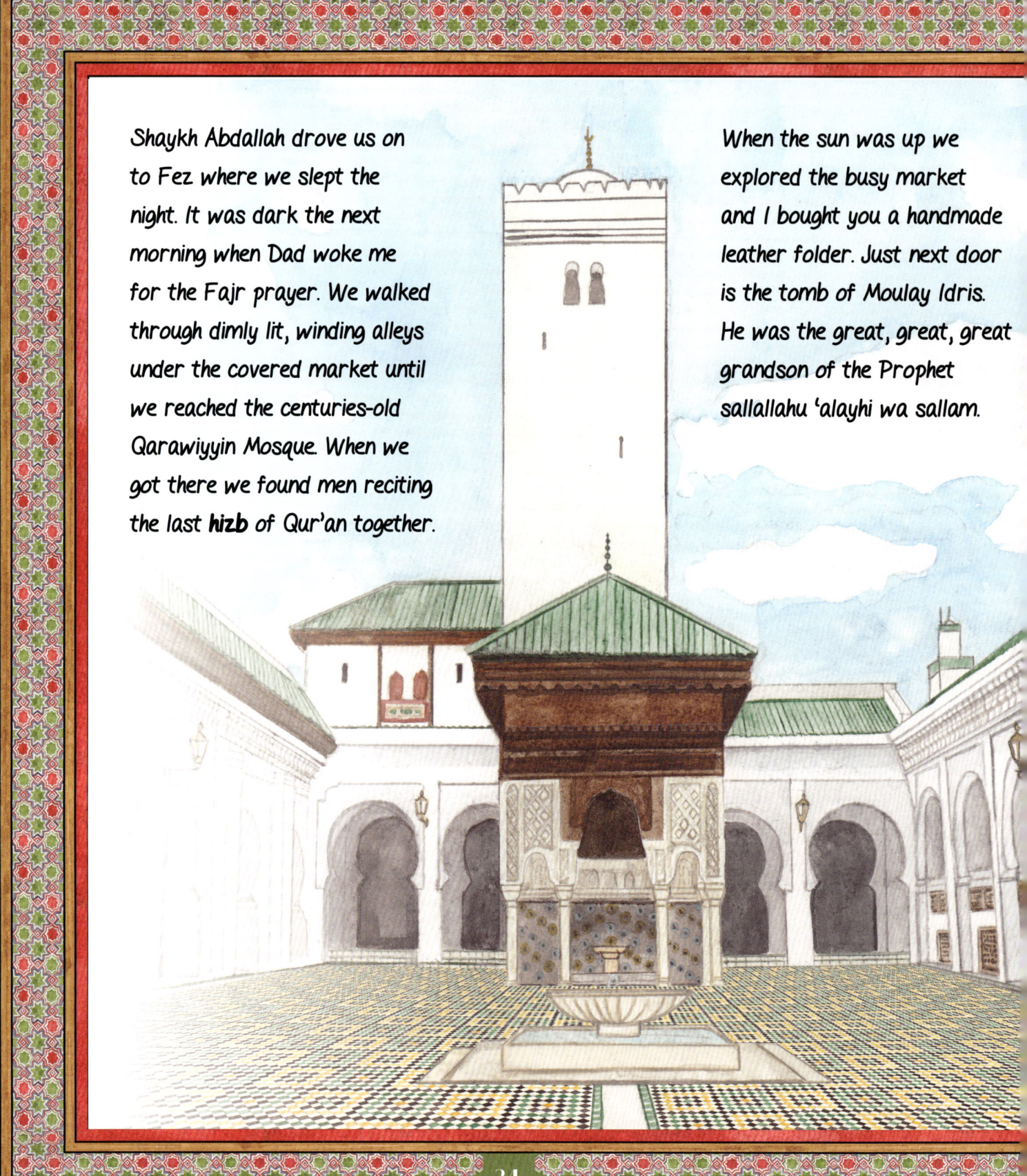

Shaykh Abdallah drove us on to Fez where we slept the night. It was dark the next morning when Dad woke me for the Fajr prayer. We walked through dimly lit, winding alleys under the covered market until we reached the centuries-old Qarawiyyin Mosque. When we got there we found men reciting the last **hizb** of Qur'an together.

When the sun was up we explored the busy market and I bought you a handmade leather folder. Just next door is the tomb of Moulay Idris. He was the great, great, great grandson of the Prophet sallallahu 'alayhi wa sallam.

We drove on to Marrakesh. All along the road we saw little cafés offering flaky pancakes you can eat with honey, and **tagines** of delicious stews served with fresh flat bread. You can just park your car and eat! Dad and I loved it so much we bought you a tagine and managed to find a Moroccan cookbook in English. But the gift I know you're going to like best is the fancy **jallaba** I chose for you.

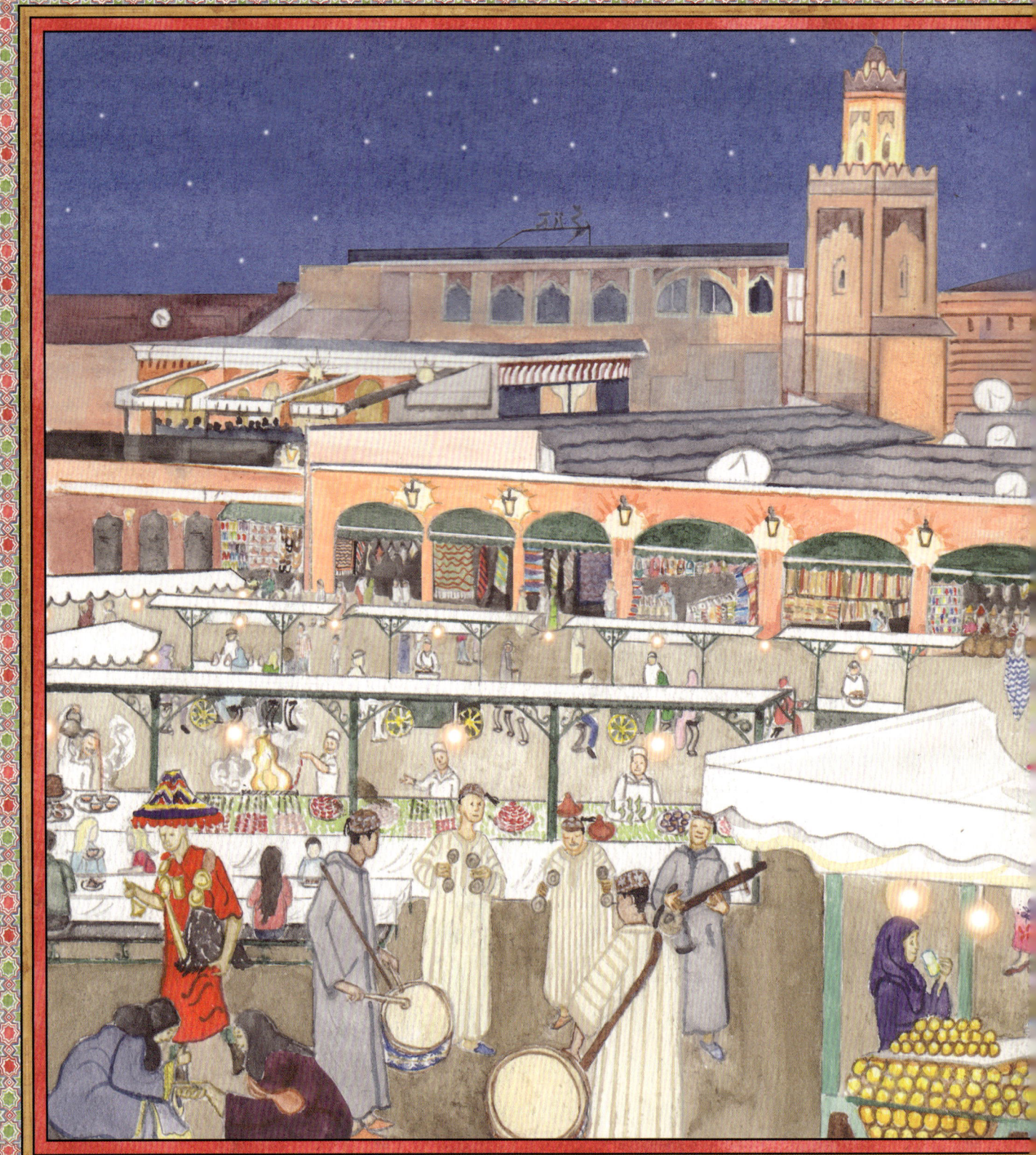

When we arrived at **Sidi** Ahmad's house it was late in the night but his whole family had stayed up for us. They served us some food and asked us lots of questions about our trip. The next day we went to Shaykh Jazuli's tomb where they were reciting the prayer on the Prophet, sallallahu 'alayhi wa sallam. That evening we went to Jama Fana which has an incredible food market. We had a great time tasting harira, grilled meats and all kinds of olives.

There were snake charmers, fire throwers and lots of musicians who were competing to be heard. Dad sat talking to his friend until I couldn't keep awake, then we took a taxi back to the house.

The next day we went on a tour through the narrow lanes of the city, stopping at mosques and ancient buildings to visit the tombs of the **Sabat Rijal, or 'the seven honoured men'**.

Eid Mubarak! Our **Eid** has been so different to home. The night before it was already festive - the streets were bustling and we could hear singing and music being played everywhere. I noticed that the air smelt of sweetmeats and rose water.

On Eid morning we walked to the mosque for the Eid prayer. The streets were full of people making their way there. Afterwards we were invited to a farm to celebrate. Wrestling matches and horse riding competitions were held and everyone had such a good time. Later in the day I was so exhausted I fell asleep on the sofa!

We're on our way home now. I'm quite sad our trip is ending but I can't wait to show you the photos I took and tell you more stories. I can hardly believe we travelled in three different continents! But everywhere we went it felt a little bit like home, and I think it's because there was a feeling of love between everyone we spent time with. In fact, Dad and I have invited everyone to visit! See you soon...

Love, Adnan

MANGO LASSI

Ingredients

1/3 cup mango pulp

2/3 cup yoghurt

2/3 cup milk

2 teaspoons sugar

3 ice cubes

Pistachio nuts, chopped

Gold leaf

Method

Blend all ingredients

Add ice

Decorate with pistachios and gold leaf

STUFFED APRICOTS

Ingredients

2 tablespoons honey

1 cup warm water

Dried Turkish apricots

Dates, chopped into small pieces

Pine nuts

Icing sugar

Whipping cream

Method

Make a syrup by mixing the warm water and honey

Soak the apricots in the syrup for 1 hour, then drain

Mix together the dates and pistachio nuts

Press the mixture into the apricots

Place on a plate and dust with icing sugar

Top with spoonfuls of whipped cream

Decorate with pine nuts

ORANGE SALAD

Ingredients

3 oranges, peeled and sliced

1 red onion, finely sliced

Cinnamon powder

Salt, a few pinches

Parsley, a handful

1 lemon, juice

Method

Arrange half of the orange slices on plate

Sprinkle with salt and cinnamon

Add half of the onion slices

Repeat layers

Garnish with chopped parsley

Squeeze a little lemon juice on top

ORANGE BLOSSOM BISCUITS

Ingredients

500g salted butter

250g caster sugar

250g corn flour

100g ground almonds

1 tsp orange blossom water

1kg plain flour

Method

Cream the butter and sugar until pale

Whisk in the corn flour, almonds and fragrant water

Stir in the plain flour and form a dough

Shape into 30 flattened 5cm-wide balls

Place on a greased baking tray

Bake for 20 minutes at 180°

Remove from tray and cool on a rack

GLOSSARY

Page 9.

tuk tuk: a three-wheeled motorised vehicle used as a taxi

naan: in Indian cooking, a type of leavened bread which is traditionally cooked in a clay oven

lassi: a sweet or savory Indian drink made from yoghurt

12.

dhikr: literally 'remembrance'. Commonly used, it means the remembering of Allah either alone or in a group

Qawwali: a type of dhikr popular in the Indian sub-continent

13.

Sallallahu 'alayhi wa sallam: 'Allah's blessing on him and peace.' This expression is said after mention of the Prophet Muhammad

Urdu: a widely used language originating in India and derived from Persian, Arabic and Hindustani

14.

Chandni Chawk: literally means 'Moonlight Square' because it was originally divided by canals to reflect the moonlight. It is now described as one of the largest and oldest markets in India

Moghul: the Muslim dynasty of Mongol origin founded by the successors of Tamerlane, which ruled much of India from the 16th to the 19th century

waqaf: an income or form of property donated for a charitable purpose, which cannot be given away or sold to anyone, for all time

15.

Nizamuddin Auliya (1238 - 1325): a famous Sufi saint (wali)

Fatiha: the opening chapter of The Noble Qur'an

18.

Ceylon: modern day Sri Lanka

mithai: traditional Indian sweets

burfi: a traditional Indian sweet made from milk solids or condensed milk, and other ingredients like ground cashew or pistachio nuts

21.

Fajr: the dawn Prayer, and the first of the five daily Prayers

adhan: the call to Prayer

Companions: as in the Companions of the Prophet, Allah's blessing on him and peace. If a Muslim saw the Prophet or talked to him at least once when the Prophet was alive, he or she is referred to as a Companion, or 'Sahabi'

23.

Mimar Sinan (1490 - 1588): the greatest architect in the Ottoman Empire and a civil engineer

25.

Sahaba: Companions of the Prophet

GLOSSARY  (CONTINUED)

26.

Bosphorus: a strait that connects the Black Sea with the Sea of Marmara and separates Europe from the Anatolian peninsula of western Asia. Istanbul is located at its south end

27.

calligrapher: someone who practices the art of decorative handwriting or lettering with a pen or brush

28.

Shaykh: a leader in a Muslim community or a spiritual teacher

Ummah: the Muslims worldwide, as one distinct Community

29.

Jalal ad-Din Rumi: a famous Sufi saint, poet, jurist, scholar and theologian of the 13th century CE. He lived and died in Konya, Turkey

Dervishes: a Sufi order who, as part of their spiritual practice, twirl around while repeating the Divine Name - Allah. Also known as 'whirling Dervishes'

33.

wali: literally 'friend', and in this context someone who is a 'friend' of Allah, a saint

Lalla: Lady. A title given to a woman of noble or royal background

qasida: a song sung in Arabic glorifying Allah and praising the Prophet, Muhammad

34.

hizb: a 60th portion of The Noble Qur'an

35.

tagine: a North African stew of spiced meat and vegetables prepared by slow cooking in a shallow earthenware cooking dish with a tall, conical lid

jellaba: a loose, hooded robe traditionally worn by Arabs

37.

Sidi: Mr, or Sir. A term of respect given to a man

Sabat Rijal, or 'the seven honoured men': outstanding men of great knowledge, learning and teaching of Islam

38.

Eid: the festival at the end of the fast of Ramadan, held on the first day of the lunar month called Shawwal

Eid Mubarak: a greeting which means 'may your festival be blessed'

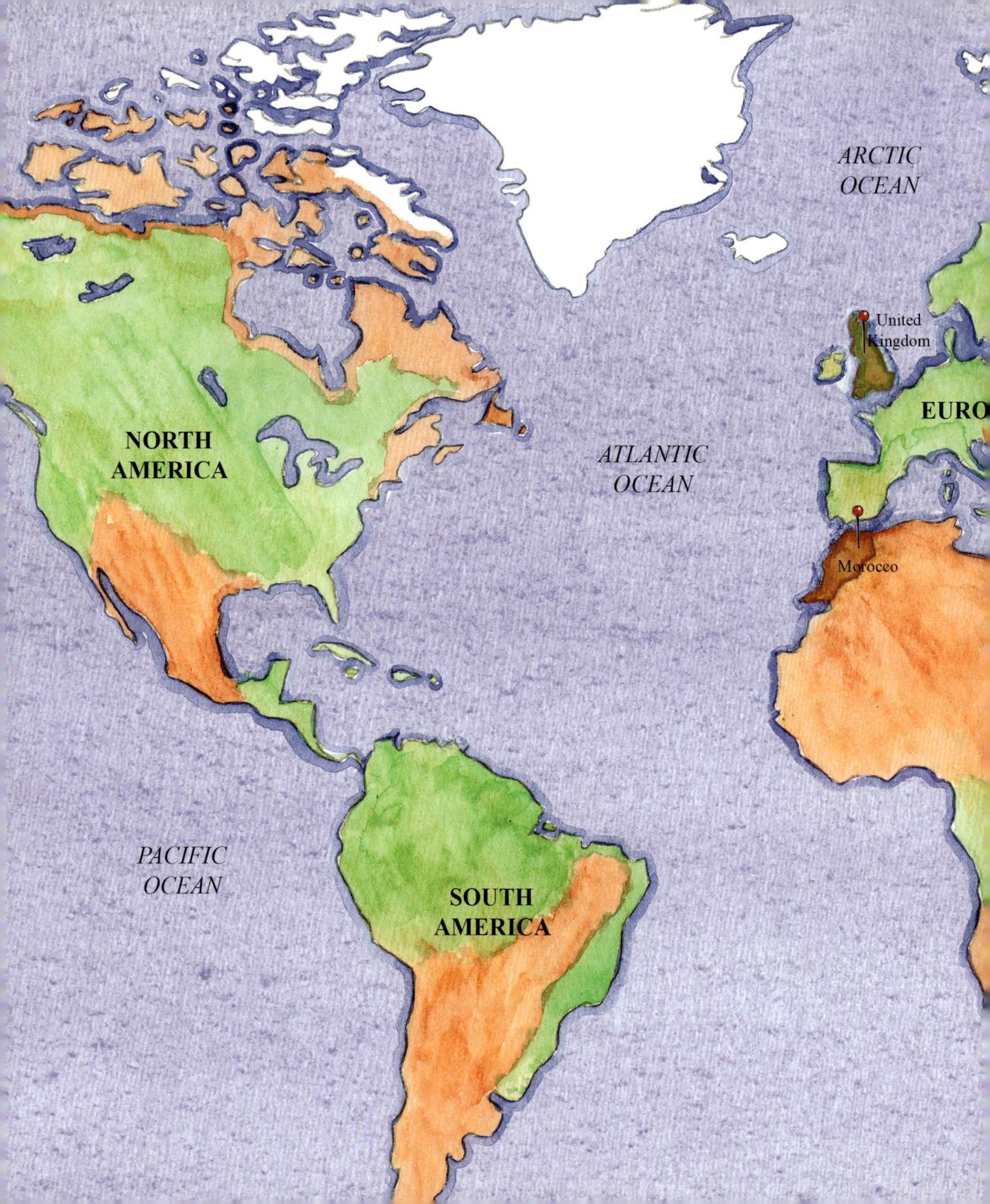